RAF, DOMINION & ALLIED SQUADRONS AT WAR:
STUDY, HISTORY AND STATISTICS

COMPILED BY
PHIL H. LISTEMANN

Drawings by Claveworks Graphic

I0167779

PREFACE

The purpose of this study is to provide aviation historians and enthusiasts with a range of information relative to each of the Commonwealth squadrons that saw combat during World War II. Each record will comprise a short history, complete with illustrations and artwork, and accompanied by the following appendices:

Appendix I: Squadron Commanders and Flight Commanders
Appendix II: Major awards
Appendix III: Operational diary (number of sorties per month)
Appendix IV: Victory list
Appendix V: Aircraft losses on operations
Appendix VI: Aircraft losses in accidents
Appendix VII: Aircraft Serial numbers matching with individual letters (including mission totals for multi-engine aircraft)
Appendix VIII: Nominal roll (Captains only for bomber and seaplane units)
Appendix IX: Roll of Honour

Individual files will be constantly updated, when any fresh information comes to light. Additional information will be available for download, at no charge, on each squadron's site at:

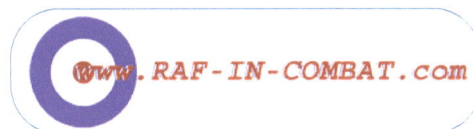

www.RAF-IN-COMBAT.com

GLOSSARY OF TERMS

RANKS

AC: Aircraftman
G/C: Group Captain
W/C: Wing Commander
S/L: Squadron Leader
F/L: Flight Lieutenant
F/O: Flying Officer
P/O: Pilot Officer
W/O: Warrant Officer
F/Sgt: Flight Sergeant
Sgt: Sergeant
Cpl: Corporal
LAC: Leading Aircraftman

OTHER

AAF: Auxiliary Air Force
CO: Commanding Officer
DFC: Distinguished Flying Cross

DFM: Distinguished Flying Medal
DSO: Distinguished Service Order
Eva.: Evaded
Inj.: Injured
ORB: Operational Record Book
OTU: Operational Training Unit
PAF: Polish Air Force
PoW: Prisoner of War
RAF: Royal Air Force
RAAF: Royal Australian Air Force
RCAF: Royal Canadian Air Force
RNZAF: Royal New Zealand Air Force
SAAF: South African Air Force
Sqn: Squadron
TOC: Taken on charge
†: Killed

No. 128 Squadron 1941-1945

ISBN: 978-2918590-68-2

Contributors & Acknowledgments:
Hugh Halliday, Paul Sortehaug, Roger Wallsgrove (Text consultant)

Cover: Hurricane BD776/WG-F flying over Western African landscape in 1941.

MAIN EQUIPMENT

HURRICANE I	Oct.41 - Mar.43
HURRICANE II	Oct.41 - Mar.43
SPITFIRE IV	Oct.42 - Nov.42
MOSQUITO XX	Sep.44 - Nov.44
MOSQUITO XXV	Oct.44 - Nov.44
MOSQUITO XVI	Oct.44 - Sep.45

SQUADRON CODE LETTERS:

WG

(WESTERN AFRICA - HURRICANE MK.I/II, DISCONTINUED BY MID-42)

M5

(EUROPE - MOSQUITO)

SQUADRON HISTORY

No.128 Squadron was reformed on **7 October 1941**[1] and unlike all the other RAF squadrons, its formation was not to fight against the Germans, but against the French Vichy forces. Indeed, it was formed from the Defense Flight of No.95 Squadron based at Hastings in Sierra Leone. The British colony was surrounded by suspect and almost hostile French Vichy possessions and the British were concerned that French airstrips might be used temporarily by the *Luftwaffe*. During 1941 many reconnaissance flights had been carried out by the French, obliging the British to form a fighter Flight during summer 1941, which had met some successes against French aircraft. The unit soon proved not enough to cover the large area, and it was decided to expand the Flight into a full squadron with the responsibility of the defense of the bases and ports of West Africa.

The squadron took time to reach the full squadron status, and the build up was slow, usually diverting pilots from the ferry flight pool based at Takoradi and aircraft from the Middle East transport route. Experienced personnel arrived to lead the squadron, including the new CO, S/L Billy Drake, but when the latter shot down another French aircraft on 13 December 1941, the squadron was not fully operational, comprising of only a single flight. It had to wait May 1942 to see its second flight formed and have its full complement of aircraft and personnel. After having lost an aircraft in December 1941, the French became more cautious and flights over the British colony were more scattered. However, the squadron remained vigilant and many scrambles were carried out, generally to intercept friendly aircraft. In 1942, the squadron began to carry out reconnaissance sorties over French territory, most of the time over Conakry (French Guinea) with locally modified Hurricanes with cameras. At the same time, a detachment was sent in Gambia, but air activity remained at a low level except during autumn 1942, when the British were worried about the possible reaction of the French Vichy forces after the Allied landings in North Africa in November 1942. Many operational flights were carried out, including a handful with one Spifire Mk.IV, but the French forces in the area joined the Allies subsequently without major problems. Considering the new strategic situation in the Western Africa, the existence of the squadon became obviously a nonsense and logically its disbandment was pronounced on 8 March 1943.

On 5 September 1944, No.128 Squadron was reformed for the second time in the United Kingdom at Wyton, as a Mosquito light-bomber unit of No.8 (Pathfinder) Group of Bomber Command. Operations began five days later when one Mosquito bombed Berlin. During the remainder of the war in Europe, the squadron was deeply involved in Bomber Command raids and became a very efficient unit. At VE-Day, the squadron had completed 1,500 sorties for the loss of over 20 Mosquitoes including four in the same night (14/15 January 1945). The squadron's crews became among the most awarded of the bomber Mosquito units, with 1 DSO, 36 DFCs and 3 DFMs. The squadron remained inside Bomber Command until 20 September 1945 when it was transferred to B.A.F.O. (British Air Forces of Occupation) and most of its wartime personnel were posted away. It then began a new career which ended in April 1946 when it became No.14 Squadron.

[1] First formed in February 1918 and disbanded the following July.

SQUADRON BASES

Hastings (Sierra Leone)	07.10.41 - 08.03.43	Wyton	05.09.44 - 22.06.45
.../...		Warboys	22.06.45 - 20.09.45

APPENDIX I
SQUADRON AND FLIGHT COMMANDERS

Rank and Name	SN	Origin	Dates
F/L John I. **KILMARTIN** (*TEMP.*)	RAF No.39793	(IRE)/RAF	07.10.41 - 14.10.41
S/L Billy **DRAKE**	RAF No.39095	RAF	14.10.41 - 27.03.42
S/L John I. **KILMARTIN**	RAF No.39793	(IRE)/RAF	27.03.42 - 11.08.42
S/L Humphrey a'B. **RUSSELL**	RAF No.37692	RAF	11.08.42 - 08.03.43
.../...			
W/C Richard J. **BURROUGH**	RAF No.33107	RAF	05.09.44 - 22.10.44
W/C Ernest E. **RODLEY**	RAF No.61472	RAF	13.02.45 - 01.08.45
S/L Arthur T. **BUCKLAND** (*TEMP.*)	RAF No.68169	RAF	01.08.45 - 13.09.45
W/C Robert W. **BRAY**	RAF No.113927	RAF	13.09.45 - 20.09.45

A FLIGHT

F/L John I. **KILMARTIN**	RAF No.39793	(IRE)/RAF	07.10.41 - 11.05.42
F/L Douglas M. **WHITNEY**	NZ391885	RNZAF	11.05.42 - 28.11.42
F/L Norman E. **HANCOCK**	RAF No.83266	RAF	28.11.42 - 08.03.43
.../...			
S/L Ivor G. **BROOM**	RAF No.112392	RAF	05.09.44 - 24.01.45
S/L David **GALLANDERS**	RAF No.45446	RAF	24.01.45 - 11.08.45
S/L Benjamin S.B. **JOHNSTON**	RAF No.88475	RAF	17.08.45 - 20.09.45

B FLIGHT

F/L Leonard G. **ANDERSON**	RAF No.72090	RAF	11.05.42 - 09.09.42
F/L Robert N.G. **ALLEN**	RAF No.63484	RAF	09.09.42 - 22.12.42
F/L Dennis A. **EDWARDS**	RAF No.110575	RAF	13.01.43 - 08.03.43
.../...			
S/L Robert C. **ALABASTER**	RAF No.81065	RAF	05.09.44 - 24.11.44
S/L Ronald F.L. **TONG** (†)	RAF No.63848	RAF	24.11.44 - 10.01.45
S/L William E.G. **HUMPREYS**	RAF No.127889	RAF	10.01.45 - 24.06.45
S/L Arthur T. **BUCKLAND**	RAF No.68169	RAF	06.07.45 - 20.09.45

APPENDIX II
MAJOR AWARDS

DSO: 1
Ernest John **SAUNDERS** (No.108139 - RAF)

DFC: 37
including 5 first Bar (*) and 1 second Bar (**)
Robert Neil Greig **ALLEN** (No.63484 - RAF)
Guy Stuart **BATCHELOR** (No.174775 - RAF)
Michael Henry Astolf Topham **BAYON** (No.188908 - RAF)
Ivor Gordon **BROOM** (No.112392 - RAF)**
Thomas John **BROOM** (No.51227 - RAF)*
Richard James **BURROUGH** (No.33107 - RAF)
Basil Martin **BUSH** (No.101038 - RAF)
Trevor Netherton **BUTCHER** (No.169481 - RAF)

Miles Richard John **Chetwynd-Stapylton** (No.102064 - RAF)
Eric William Bengrey **Denton** (Aus.1997 - RAAF)
Patrick James **Duncan** (No.83994 - RAF)
Robert May **Dwerryhouse** (NZ411868 - RNZAF)
Thomas Arthur **Empson** (NZ414606 - RNZAF)
John Seymour **Etherington** (No.130645 - RAF)
Ian James **Fawcett** (Aus.409101 - RAAF)
David **Gallanders** (No.45446 - RAF)
John **Harbottle** (No.141809 - RAF)*
Arthur Eustace **Hutchinson** (No.115585 - RAF)
Byron Thomas Stephen **Jones** (No.137095 - RAF)
William **Lane** (No.972649 - RAF)
James Hamilton **Leckenby** (Can./J.43893 - RCAF)
Alan Johnson **Mayfield** (NZ417084 - RNZAF)
William Thew **Mayson** (No.148757 - RAF)*
Bruce Davidson **McEwan** (Can./J.38574 - RCAF)
George Patrick **Mullan** (No.132984 - RAF)
Arthur Edward **Parry** (Aus.406661 - RAAF)
Archibald William **Robinson** (No.150114 - RAF)
Jonathan Chester **Schwandt** (Can./J.94302 - RCAF)
John William Gainer **Smith** (No.134129 - RAF)
Leicester George **Smith** (NZ414352 - RNZAF)
Stanley Robert **Stanbridge** (No.134653 - RAF)*
Douglas Hereward **Swain** (Aus.410791 - RAAF)
James Scott **Walker** (No.118970 - RAF)*
Edward Peter **Wallace** (No.133403 - RAF)
Robert George **Webster** (NZ412293 - RNZAF)
Leo Charles Raymond **Wellstead** (No.133927 - RAF)
Anthony Edwin **Willey** (No.159877 - RAF)

DFM: 3
Andrew **Brown** (No.530644 - RAF)
Douglas **Harper** (No.1572305 - RAF)
William Charles **Parker** (No.1802388 - RAF)

APPENDIX III
OPERATIONAL DIARY
NUMBER OF SORTIES PER MONTH

Date	Month	Total		Date	Month	Total
Dec.41	2	*2*				
Jan.42	32	*34*				
Feb.42	15	*49*		Sep.44	22	*323*
Mar.42	18	*67*		Oct.44	184	*507*
Apr.42	17	*84*		Nov.44	167	*674*
May.42	23	*107*		Dec.44	199	*873*
Jun.42	6	*113*		Jan.45	135	*1,008*
Jul.42	10	*123*		Feb.45	209	*1,217*
Aug.42	12	*135*		Mar.45	273	*1,490*
Sep.42	6	*141*		Apr.45	246	*1,736*
Oct.42	43	*184*		May.45	16	*1,752*
Nov.42	65	*249*				
Dec.42	17	*266*		**Grand Total**		**1,752**
Jan.43	35	*301*				
.../...						

Extracted from AIR27/932

APPENDIX IV
VICTORY LIST
CONFIRMED (C) AND PROBABLE (P) CLAIMS

Date	Pilot	SN	Origin	Type	Serial	Code	Nb	Cat.

HURRICANE II

Date	Pilot	SN	Origin	Type	Serial	Code	Nb	Cat.
13.12.41	S/L Billy **DRAKE**	RAF No.39095	RAF	M-167F	**BP897**	WG-P	1.0	C

Total: 1.0
Aircraft damaged: -

APPENDIX V
AIRCRAFT LOST ON OPERATIONS

Date	Pilot	S/N	Origin	Serial	Code	Mark	Fate

HURRICANE

Date	Pilot	S/N	Origin	Serial	Code	Mark	Fate
10.05.42	P/O Arthur G. **TODD**	RAF No.119873	RAF	**Z5340**		IIB	-

Took off at 07.20 as No.2 to S/L Kilmartin to carry out a recce over Vichy French territory. For unspecified reasons, Todd was obliged to make a force landing in British territory. Todd was later picked up at 12.30. The aircraft was not repaired and struck off charge on 30.05.42. Arthur Todd served at first with No.245 Sqn in Europe before being sent to Malta in May the same year where he joined No.261 Sqn. He remained a short time there and was posted to West Africa to ferry Tomahawks to Egypt. The need for fighter pilots in West Africa meant that he was posted to No.95 Sqn Defense flight with which he shot down a VichyFrench M167 on 22 August 1941. He joined No.128 Sqn on formation. He returned to the UK in later in the year 1942 and subsequently served with No.56 Sqn on Typhoons and then with No.164 Sqn on Hurricane IVs. At the end of the war, he led No.257 Sqn (January – March 1945). He retired as Wing Commander in 1958.
Note on the aircraft: TOC No.20 MU 20.08.41, sailed for Middle East 03.09.41.

SPITFIRE

Date	Pilot	S/N	Origin	Serial	Code	Mark	Fate
28.11.42	F/L Robert N.G. **ALLEN**	RAF No.63484	RAF	**BR642**		IV	-

Taking off for an operational flight at 12.30, F/L Allen saw one of the tyre burst. The Spitfire swung and the undercarriage collapsed due to the rough surface on the runway. F/L Allen was among the original pilots of the squadron and was with the squadron for more than a year and was a formerly with No.95 Sqn Defense Flight with which he flew from July 1941 onwards.
Note on the aircraft: TOC No.1 PRU 18.06.42. Arrived Takoradi 27.10.42.

MOSQUITO

Date	Pilot	S/N	Origin	Serial	Code	Mark	Fate
17.09.44	F/O Hugh J. **BARTLEY**	Can./J.17039	RCAF	**KB210**	M5-P	XX	**Inj.**
	Sgt John L. **HARTLEY**	RAF No.954358	RAF				†

KB210 was the only aircraft to take off that night with Brunswick as target, departing at 00.29. Bomber Command had the mission to support Operation 'Market Garden'. No.128 Sqn was part of a larger formation containing 33 bomber Mosquitoes with targets Brunswick and Dortmunt. It was the only bomber Mosquito lost that night which saw also the loss of 2 Lancasters. It seems that the aircraft lost control over Belgium at 25,000 feet and when the aircraft broke up at low altitude, the pilot was able to evacuate the Mosquito but Hartley fell to his death with the aircraft. The crew had joined the squadron on re-formation and was completing its second sortie since then. Bartley, a Canadian from Manitoba, was slightly injured and taken to a US Army Hospital. He survived the war and served with the RCAF after the war.

Note on the aircraft: Built in Canada, it arrived in UK on 30.04.44. Served with No.1655 MTU. Date unrecorded but believed to have joined the squadron on formation. Lost returning from its 6th mission (one aborted). [nbr missions completed: 5].

| 30.10.44 | F/O Kenneth H. **KING** | RAF No.149202 | RAF | **KB199** | M5-A | XX | † |
| | F/O Cecil M. **ARRIETTA** | RAF No.155919 | RAF | | | | **PoW** |

Eleven squadron Mosquitoes were detailed that night with Berlin as target, KB199 taking off at 19.49. No.128 Sqn was part of a larger formation containing 62 bomber Mosquitoes. KB199 was one of two Bomber Command Mosquitoes lost that night, which were the only losses sustained by the Command that night. Kenneth King had been awarded the **DFC** while serving with No.78 Sqn and F/O Arrietta his **DFM** while serving with No.10 Sqn and had arrived the previous day. They were completing their first sortie for No.128 Sqn.

Note on the aircraft: Built in Canada, it arrived in UK on 12.08.44. Served with No.1655 MTU before being issued to No.128 Sqn 22.09.44. Lost on its 17th mission. [nbr missions completed: 15].

| 04.11.44 | F/O Edward P. **WALLACE** | RAF No.133403 | RAF | **MM197** | M5-P | XVI | † |
| | Sgt Robert A. **SOUTAR** | RAF No.1672449 | RAF | | | | † |

Eleven Mosquitoes were detailed that night with Berlin as target, MM197 taking off at 23.33. On return an engine failed and while approaching to land a wingtip brushed the ground causing the Mosquito to cartwheel and crash at 05.02 just short of the runway near a bulk fuel store. Wallace was taken to hospital where he died. No.128 Sqn was part of a larger formation containing 64 bomber Mosquitoes and this was the only loss of the raid. Wallace was later awarded the **DFC** gazetted in January 1945. Edward Wallace, 21, and Soutar, a Scot of 23, were returning from their 8th sortie since they joined the squadron in October. Edward Wallace's older brother, John Wallace, Lieutenant in the Life Guards, also died in service in August 1946.

Note on the aircraft: Built by De Havilland, it served first with No.109 Sqn before being issued to No.128 Sqn at an unrecorded date. Lost returning from its 2nd mission. [nbr missions completed: 2].

| 06.11.44 | F/L Jack L. **ELLIS** | RAF No.39510 | RAF | **KB353** | M5-Z | XX | † |
| | Sgt Donald W. **BRITTAN** | RAF No.1587323 | RAF | | | | † |

Ten squadron Mosquitoes were detailed that night with Gelsenkirchen as target, KB353 taking off at 18.15. Lost without trace. No.128 Sqn was part of a larger formation containing 48 bomber Mosquitoes. It was the only bomber Mosquito lost that night which saw also the loss of 13 other aircraft of Bomber Command. The crew had been with the squadron for a couple of days, and was completing its first sortie for the unit.

Note on the aircraft: Built in Canada, it arrived in UK on 20.07.44. Served with Nos.608 and 139 Sqns before being issued to No.128 Sqn on 13.09.44. Lost during its 11th mission. Carried out the first successful sortie of No.128 Sqn on the night 10/11.09.44 with S/L Broom and F/L Broom as a crew. [nbr missions completed: 10].

| 15.11.44 | F/L John S. **ETHERINGTON** | RAF No.130645 | RAF | **MM196** | M5-Q | XVI | **Inj.** |
| | F/O Sidney **HARRISON** | RAF No.171806 | RAF | | | | - |

Seven squadron Mosquitoes were detailed that night with Berlin as target, MM196 taking off at 17.07. The squadron sent a mixed force of Mosquito XX and XVI. The aircraft came down in Allied held territory but the real causes are unknown. It was a minor raid of 36 bomber Mosquitoes escorted by RCM aircraft and intruders, and this was the only loss of the raid. Even if they both joined the squadron in September 1944, they weren't regular crewmembers, as though it was the 15th operational flight for Etherington, it was only the third with F/O Harrison for whom it was his 9th. Etherington used to fly with F/O Henry Crumplin **DFM** while F/O Harrison flew with F/L Charles Owen. Etherington returned to the squadron in March and completed 15 more missions with a new navigator, Sgt Arthur Rhodes. Etherington was posted to No.571 Sqn in September 1945 with Harrison, who seems not to have flown anymore with the squadron after this accident.

Note on the aircraft: Built by De Havilland, it served first with No.109 Sqn before being issued to No.128 Sqn 31.10.44. Lost returning from its 12th mission. [nbr missions completed: 11].

| 23.11.44 | F/O George W. **TUCK** | Aus.408938 | RAAF | **MM201** | M5-Y | XVI | † |
| | Sgt Maurice H. **MOSS** | RAF No.1686131 | RAF | | | | † |

Twelve squadron Mosquitoes were detailed that night with Hannover as target, MM201 taking off at 16.57. Lost without trace. No.128 Sqn was part of a bomber Mosquito raid of 82 aircraft with 43 other aircraft supporting the raid and MM201 became the only loss of the raid. George Tuck, an Australian from Victoria, and Moss, had been with the squadron for a month. It was the first operational tour for Tuck who had served in various flying instructor postings between 1942 and 1944. They were posted missing on their 8th sortie.

Note on the aircraft: Built by De Havilland, issued to No.128 Sqn 02.11.44. Lost returning from its 3rd mission. [nbr missions completed: 2].

| 26.11.44 | F/O Herbert E. **BOULTER** | RAF No.174875 | RAF | **MM203** | M5-U | XVI | - |
| | Sgt James R. **CHURCHER** | RAF No.1803850 | RAF | | | | - |

Eleven squadron Mosquitoes were detailed that night with Nurnberg as target, MM203 taking off at 01.02. Returning to base, an engine failed and the crew was ordered to bale out near Calais (France). Both airmen were picked up by the Royal Navy and returned safely to the squadron. It was a bomber Mosquito raid of 87 aircraft supported by 38 Intruder Mosquitoes and 36 RCM aircraft. MM203 was the only Bomber Command loss of that raid. The crew had just completed their 10th sortie and resumed operations within the next fortnight. Churcher continued to fly with Boulter during 9 more sorties but seems to have stopped flying operational sorties in January 1945. He eventually left the squadron at the end of his tour in March 1945. (see operational loss 14.01.45)

Note on the aircraft: Built by De Havilland, it served first with No.109 Sqn before being issued to No.128 Sqn 05.11.44. Lost returning from its 2nd mission. [nbr missions completed: 1].

| 28.11.44 | W/O Frank **EDGAR** | RAF No.1026434 | RAF | **MM195** | M5-A | XVI | † |
| | Sgt Joseph H.M. **MURPHY** | Can./R.185419 | RCAF | | | | † |

Ten squadron Mosquitoes were detailed that night with Nurnberg as target, MM195 taking off at 17.25. Lost without trace. No.128 Sqn was part of a larger formation containing 84 bomber Mosquitoes. It was the only Bomber Command loss that night, from over 620 sorties. Having joined the squadron in October and on his 8th sortie, Joseph Murphy, from the province of Quebec, had been sent overseas in April 1944. He was commissioned the previous day as J.95450 but was still awaiting notification.

Note on the aircraft: Built by De Havilland, it was issued to No.128 Sqn 15.10.44. Lost on its 7th mission. [nbr missions completed: 6].

| 11.12.44 | F/L Ronald C. **ONLEY** | RAF No.102560 | RAF | **MM190** | M5-C | XVI | † |
| | F/O George B. **COLLINS** | Aus.436900 | RAAF | | | | † |

Nine squadron Mosquitoes were detailed that night with Hamburg as target, MM190 taking off at 18.12. Lost witjou trace. It was a Mosquito raid of 90 aircraft to Hamburg, Hanover, Schwerte, Bielefelt and Duisbourg, and MM190 was the only loss of the night. They were with the squadron for two days and were completing their first sortie. Collins was an English-born Australian.

Note on the aircraft: Built by De Havilland, it was issued to No.128 Sqn 05.10.44. Lost on its 21st mission. [nbr missions completed: 20].

| 01.01.45 | F/L Leo C.R. **WELLSTEAD** | RAF No.133927 | RAF | **PF411** | M5-B | XVI | † |
| | F/L George P. **MULLAN** | RAF No.132984 | RAF | | | | † |

Six squadron Mosquitoes were detailed that night with the Coblenz area and its railways tunnels as target, PF411 taking off at 06.41. It was a Mosquito day raid of 17 aircraft of No.8 Group to bomb the mouths of tunnels in the wooded and hilly Eiffel region between the Rhine and the Ardennes battle area. The Mosquito carried a 4,000-lb bomb. PF411 crashed on take-off due to engine failure, killing both crew. The rest of the formation completed the raid successfully with 14 tunnels attacked and PF411 was the only one not to participate. Wellstead was flying with a DFM awarded during a previous tour with No.99 Sqn flying Wellingtons. Both were awarded the DFC gazetted in March and February respectively. This crew had joined the squadron in the UK from the beginning and had carried out their first sortie on the night of 10/11 September over Berlin. It was their 27th sortie for the squadron.

Note on the aircraft: Built by Percival, it was first issued to No.105 Sqn on 02.11.44 before being issued to No.128 Sqn at an unrecorded date. Lost taking-off for its 26th mission. [nbr missions completed: 25].

| 10.01.45 | S/L Ronald F.L. **Tong** | RAF No.63848 | RAF | **PF403** | M5-T | XVI | † |
| | F/L Marc J.M. **Lagesse** | RAF No.128616 | RAF | | | | † |

Eleven squadron Mosquitoes were detailed that night with Hannover as target, PF403 taking off at 17.07. The aircraft crashed on return, after having been told to stand by due to poor visibility and a snow storm. The message was acknowledged by the crew and while circling the aerodrome it was seen banking steeply, out of control. It crashed into Cambridge Road, Godmanchester. This was a Mosquito raid of 50 aircraft and it was the only loss. The crew had joined the squadron at the end of November posted from No.139 Sqn. S/L Tong had been awarded the DFC on a previous tour with No.57 Sqn, while Marc Lagesse, from Mauritius received his DFC with No.139 Sqn while flying Mosquitoes. His DFC was gazetted after his death, however, on 27.02.45.

Note on the aircraft: Built by Percival, it was issued to No.128 Sqn on 09.10.44 (but received on 20.10.44). Lost returning from its 33ʳᵈ mission.[*nbr missions completed: 32*].

| 14.01.45 | F/O Alan W. **Heitmann** | Aus.409918 | RAAF | **MM194** | M5-K | XVI | † |
| | P/O Arthur N. **Gould** | RAF No.188552 | RAF | | | | - |

Thirteen squadron Mosquitoes were detailed that night with Berlin as target, MM194 taking off at 21.00, No.128 Sqn being part of a diversionary sweep of 83 to the German capital. A deadly raid for the squadron which lost four aircraft that night, but the main and diversionary raid were costly as well due enemy action but also because of bad weather. In all Bomber Command lost 14 Lancasters, 3 Halifaxes, 1 Liberator and 10 Mosquitoes in over 1,200 sorties. MM194 ran out of fuel and was partially abandoned after several attempts to land returning from the mission. Indeed they were given instructions to abandon the aircraft, the navigator doing so from 1,500 feet and P/O Gould parachuted safely, but the pilot later reported the aircraft being out of control. The aircraft crashed at 02.34, the 15ᵗʰ near Chatteris, Cambridgeshire with F/O Heitmann sitll on board. Alan Heitmann was an Australian from Victoria, who was posted to No.128 Sqn at the end of September as being his first operational posting, while Gould continued to fly in operations until April 1945 at the end of his tour. They did not usually fly together, as Alan Heitman used to fly with F/L Ian Fawcett (RAAF), the bombing leader of the squadron.

Note on the aircraft: Built by De Havilland, it was issued to No.128 Sqn 12.10.44. Lost returning from its 22ⁿᵈ mission.[*nbr missions completed: 21*].

| | F/O Douglas H. **Swain** | Aus.410791 | RAAF | **PF401** | M5-G | XVI | - |
| | P/O Michael H.A.T. **Bayon** | RAF No.188908 | RAF | | | | - |

See above. PF401 took off at 21.02 and was lost on landing back to base at 02.02, the 15ᵗʰ overshooting the runway, the crew escaping injuries. Being short of fuel and with the weather deteriorating, Swain decided to rush the landing and seems not have taken all needed precautions. Swain was an Australian from Victoria and had joined No.128 Sqn at the end of October 44 as his first posting. He was later posted to No.162 sqn (March 45 – May 45) and in all was reported to have completed 44 sorties with No.128 Sqn and 4 more with No.162 Sqn. He was awarded the DFC, while Bayon will be awarded in July 1945 for his service for the squadron.

Note on the aircraft: Built by Percival, it was issued to No.128 Sqn on 05.10.44 Lost returning from its 34ᵗʰ mission.[*nbr missions completed: 33*].

| | F/O Treless A.L. **Adam** | RAF No.150225 | (Aus)/RAF | **PF404** | M5-H | XVI | † |
| | F/Sgt Alan J. **Casey** | Aus.432482 | RAAF | | | | † |

See above. PF404 had took off at 21.01 but the left engine failed shortly after take-off and the aircraft crashed three minutes later at Woodhurst, 5m N.E. of Huntington, killing the crew which had been with the squadron since November. F/O Adam and F/Sgt Casey were both Australians, Adam from Victoria while Casey was from New South Wales.

Note on the aircraft: Built by Percival, it was issued to No.128 Sqn on 13.10.44. Lost on taking-off for its 28ᵗʰ mission.[*nbr missions completed: 27*].

| | F/O Herbert E. **Boulter** | RAF No.174875 | RAF | **PF437** | M5-A | XVI | - |
| | Sgt Cecil **Hart** | RAF No.1583265 | RAF | | | | - |

See above. PF437 had taken off at 21.06. The aircraft ran out of fuel and was successfully abandoned at 02.16 from 7,000 feet and under CO instructions. Boulter was flying with C. Hart for the last three flights and had added 10 more sorties since 26ᵗʰ November before that day. Hart had been the navigator of F/P Michael Solomon with whom he had flown half a dozen missions. Neither Boulter nor Hart seem to have subsequently flown on operations with the squadron but Boulter was awarded the DFC for his service with No.163 Sqn while Hart a DFM also for for his service with No.163 Sqn, suggesting that both were posted to that unit a couple of weeks later. (see operational losses 26.11.44).

Note on the aircraft: Built by Percival, it was first issued to No.105 Sqn on 11.12.44 before being issued to No.128 Sqn on 02.01.45. Lost on its first mission.

| 04.02.45 | F/L James K. **Wood** | Aus.410777 | RAAF | **MM199** | M5-Q | XVI | † |
| | F/L Raymond **Poole** | RAF No.162285 | RAF | | | | † |

Ten squadron Mosquitoes were detailed that night with Hanover as target, MM199 taking off at 18.06. No.128 Sqn was part of 69 bomber Mosquitoes including 50 to Hanover. MM199 was hit by flak and crashed towards Benthe 9 km SW from the centre of Hanover. MM199 was the only Mosquito lost on this raid, along with 3 Lancasters. Bomber Command had sent 678 aircraft that night. It was the first operational tour for Wood who had served in various flying instructor postings between 1942 and 1944 and had joined the squadron with Poole in November 1944. He was an Australian from Victoria.

Note on the aircraft: Built by De Havilland, first issued to No.105 Sqn, then issued to No.128 Sqn 18.11.44. Lost on its 26th mission. [nbr missions completed: 25].

| 26.02.45 | F/O David W. **Rhys** | RAF No.143234 | RAF | **PF409** | M5-Z | XVI | - |
| | F/O Francis J. **Kennelly** | Can./J.43629 | RCAF | | | | - |

Ten squadron Mosquitoes were detailed that night with Erfurt as target, PF409 taking off at 18.33. No.128 Sqn was part of 69 bomber Mosquitoes including 63 to Erfurt supported by 31 RCM or Intruder aircraft, while minor operations were carried out by 30 other Bomber Command aircraft, one being lost. PF409 sustained flak damaged but was able to return to base, and after inspection, the Mosquito was written off. Francis Kennelly from British Columbia was serving overseas since May 1944 and with No.128 Sqn since December 1944 like Rhys. Kennelly was repatriated in July 1945 and eventually retired in January 1946.

Note on the aircraft: Built by De Havilland, issued to No.128 Sqn 15.11.44. SOC 17.05.45. [nbr missions completed: 43].

| 28.02.45 | F/O Neville M. **McNulty** | Aus.409062 | RAAF | **PF451** | M5-C | XVI | † |
| | F/O James R.A. **Maconachie** | Can./C.12525 | RCAF | | | | † |

Twelve squadron Mosquitoes were detailed that night with Berlin as target, PF451 taking off at 18.20. On return to base the aircraft was seen to bank steeply in trying to line up with the runway. It is believed that the pilot initiated an overshoot procedure and stalled a few seconds later at Rattlesden, 4 miles W of Stowmarket, Suffolk. This raid consisted of 98 training aircraft on a sweep over the North Sea and 86 bomber Mosquitoes to Berlin, Nuremberg and Munich and 100 other aircraft. PF451 was the only loss of the night. Neville McNulty was an Australian from Victoria, for whom it was his first operational posting, having served in various second line units in UK before joining the squadron, while James Maconachie, a regular RCAF office, was a Canadian from British Columbia and served in various bases in Canada before being posted overseas in May 1944. The crew was completing its 31st sortie since their arrival in October 1944.

Note on the aircraft: Built by Percival, it was issued to No.128 Sqn on 28.01.45. Lost returning from its 8th mission. [nbr missions completed: 7].

| 07.03.45 | S/L John D. **Armstrong** | Can./J.5707 | RCAF | **RV306** | M5-U | XVI | † |
| | F/O William E. **Whyte** | Can./J.42207 | RCAF | | | | † |

Seven squadron Mosquitoes were detailed that night with Berlin as target, RV306 taking off around 18.20. No.128 Sqn was part of a 42 Mosquito raid. The aircraft returned to base on one engine and the pilot decided to land at Gilze-Rijen airfield (Holland). It seems that the aircraft did a downwind approach and crashed while trying to go round again. It was the only loss of the raid, but Bomber Command lost also one Lancaster from 191 sent to bomb Sassnitz. Both airmen had a similar career, being Canadians from Ontario, served as flying instructors in Canada for a couple of months or years before being posted overseas, in February 1944 for Armstrong and May for Whyte. The crew was completing their 18th sortie since arriving at the squadron in October 1944.

Note on the aircraft: Built by De Havilland, it was issued to No.128 Sqn in February 1945. Lost returning from its 8th mission. [nbr missions completed: 7].

Total: 21

APPENDIX VI
AIRCRAFT LOST IN ACCIDENTS

Date	Pilot		S/N	Origin	Serial	Code	Mark	Fate

HURRICANE

24.05.42   Sgt Arthur **MARDER**   RAF No.591731   RAF   **BN223**   IIB   †

During an air test, the engine failed and smoke entered the cockpit causing the pilot to be blinded. Due to the smoke he was oblige to abandon the aircraft, which dived into the ground at Lumley Beach, Freetown, and caught fire. The true cause of the engine failure was never established, and the pilot had stated that a belly landing was totally inappropriate due to the nature of the countryside. Sadly Marder was too low to open his parachute safely and was killed. He had just joined the squadron.

Note on the aircraft:TOC No.20 MU 29.12.41.Sent to ME on SS *Katanga* 03.02.42. Arrived at Takoradi 12.03.42. NFD.

20.10.42   P/O Michael J. **AHEARNE**   RAF No.119658   RAF   **BE686**   IIB   -

During a non operational flight, the engine failed due to sediment and water in the fuel filters. The pilot was able to keep the aircraft in flight until Hastings to make a belly landing, but stalled too high and crashed. Michael Ahearne had joined the squadron a couple of weeks before and survived the war.

Note on the aircraft: TOC No.15 MU 15.11.41.Sent to ME 09.05.42. NFD.

06.11.42   F/Sgt George G. **WARREN**   Can./R.82240   RCAF   **Z2420**   IIA   -

During an air test, the engine failed obliging the pilot to make a force-landing. However due to dense clouds of smoke in the cockpit and to the nature of countryside, he decided to abandon the aircraft which dived into the ground and caught fire. Native of Ontario, Canada, Warren was serving overseas since October 1941. Later commissioned (as J16677) he was repatriated in November 1944 but was sent to the UK in March 1945 and was repatriated again in August 1945. This Hurricane was unique as it was modified locally to carry cameras located behind the cockpit (2 vertical), and always flew with extra fuel tanks under the wings, and four of its eight machine-guns deleted. It was also painted in PR-blue, soon faded out by the sun.

Note on the aircraft: TOC No.18 MU 15.11.40.Sent to ME 03.01.42. NFD.

18.11.42   Sgt James H. **CABELDU**   Can./R.99147   RCAF   **BE550**   IIB   †

Flying to Port loko in company with two others to carry out practice landings, the aircraft suddenly broke away at 600 feet below the clouds and crashed. He was not seen to crash but the wreckage was found. The cause was never determined but it is believed that he had an engine failure and caught fire in the air, lost control and spun into the ground. Native of Ontario, Canada, he was serving overseas since March 1942 and posted upon his arrival in Western Africa.

Note on the aircraft: TOC No.82 MU 24.02.42, sent to ME on SS *Biaffra* on 27.02.42. Arrived at Takoradi 12.03.42. NFD

MOSQUITO

09.12.44   F/O Alan R. **SPEIRS**   NZ413136   RNZAF   **MM198**   M5-P   XVI   -
                F/Sgt Herbert R. **CHILVERS**   Aus.434404   RAAF

F/O Speirs was proceeding for an air test when he discovered that he was unable to restart the engine after a having voluntarily feathered the propeller. Speirs decided to return to base and during the approach the Mosquito stalled at 50 feet, crashing at 12.44 near the runway. A fire broke out just after the impact, but both crew had time to escape without major injuries. Alan Speirs had flown with Nos.75 (NZ) and 7 Sqns with which he was awarded a DFC in 1944 before converting onto Mosquitoes and joined No.128 Sqn in December 1944 with Chilvers. The latter was an Australian from New South Wales who was posted to No.139 Sqn in February 1945 with which he flew 19 sorties. He was repatriated in July 1945.

Note on the aircraft: Built by De Havilland, it was issued to No.128 Sqn 02.11.44. [*nbr missions completed: 11*].

30.12.44   F/L Leonard **Gatrill**   RAF No.121939   RAF   **PF436**   XVI   -

While proceeding on the ferry flight from No.109 Sqn to No.128 Sqn, the pilot attempted to make a single-engined landing at Wyton. The aircraft stalled and hit the runway at 15.12, causing the undercarriage to collapse . The Mosquito was later declared damaged beyond repair. Gatrill was not a a pilot from No.128 Sqn.

Note on the aircraft: Built by Percival, it was issued to No.109 Sqn on 09.12.44 and issued to No.128 Sqn the day of its accident. SOC 03.07.45.

05.02.45   F/L Thomas A. **Empson**   NZ414606   RNZAF   **PF412**   M5-D   XVI   -

Crash-landed on Wyton airfield following engine failure during an air test, pilot escaping injuries. Regarding the nature of the flight, it is believed that Empson was flying alone, without his regular navigator, F/O Robert Dwerryhouse (RNZAF). The crew had joined the squadron in November 1944 and left in May 1945 for repatriation after completing 47 sorties. For Empson it was his first operational posting having served as flying instructor between July 1942 and September 1944, while Robert Dwerryhouse had previously served with 148 Sqn on Liberators in the Middle East. Both were later awarded the DFC *for having served the squadron with distinction.*

Note on the aircraft: Built by Percival, it was issued to No.109 Sqn on 04.11.44 and issued to No.128 Sqn on 26.11.44.[*nbr missions completed: 32*].

09.06.45   F/O Albert H. **Reynolds**   RAF No.172379   RAF   **PF440**   M5-H   XVI   -

Returning from a training flight, the pilot attempted to land on a short runway with a 15 knot crosswind at 45 degrees to the runway heading. He approached too high and too fast and after touchdown, used throttle to keep the aircraft straight which in turn reduced the braking effect. The aircraft overran the runway by about 100 yards and its starboard undercarriage collapsed. It was 09.50. The airframe was not repaired and became 5304M. Reynolds and his navigator, Sgt O. Adbulah, had joined the squadron in April. The presence of his navigator is unconfirmed for this flight.

Note on the aircraft: Built by Percival, it was issued to No.571 Sqn on 15.01.45 and issued to No.128 Sqn on 26.01.45. Became instructional airframe 5304M on 07.07.45. [*nbr missions completed: 45*].

13.07.45   F/O Albert H. **Reynolds**   RAF No.172379   RAF   **PF406**   M5-E   XVI   -

Shortly after tale off, the Mosquito's hydraulics system failed due to a compressor pump defect and the brakes became inoperative. The pilot decided to divert to another airfield with a longer runway and landed without brakes at 11.45. The aircraft ran for about 100 yards before a swing to the left developed and the pilot tried to correct this with use of the throttles and rudder but overcorrected and the Mosquito swung to the right, followed by the left undercarriage collapsing. It is not sure if Sgt Abdulah was on board (see previous accident details).

Note on the aircraft: Built by Percival, it was issued to RAF Upwood on 22.10.44 and issued to No.128 Sqn at an unrecorded date (around mid-November) and coded M5-W. Damaged on 23.12.44 it was repaired by De Haviland and re-issued to No.128 Sqn on 08.02.45, with the individual letter 'E'.[*nbr missions completed: 35*].

Total: 9

APPENDIX VII
Aircraft serial numbers matching with individual letters

M5-A

Z4484 *(Hurricane I as WG-A)*
BH217 *(Hurricane II - letter only)*
KB199 - [17] *(Mosquito XX)*
MM195 - [7], MM204 - [15], PF443 - [45]
(Mosquito XVI)

M5-B

Z4313 *(Hurricane I as WG-B)*
KB221 - [29] *(Mosquito XX)*
PF411 - [26], PF415 - [30], RV319 - [26]
(Mosquito XVI)

M5-C

KB363 - [14+*14 as M5-U*] *(Mosquito XX)*
MM190 - [21], PF428 - [11 + *33 as M5-D*],
PF451 - [8], PF461 - [29]
(Mosquito XVI)

M5-D

KB443 - [17] *(Mosquito XXV)*
PF412 - [32], PF428 - [33+*11 as M5-C*]
(Mosquito XVI)

M5-E

KB343 - [14] *(Mosquito XX)*
KB423 - [1] *(Mosquito XXV)*
PF406 - [22 + *13 as M5-W*],
PF410 - [16+*6 as M5-L*]
(Mosquito XVI)

M5-F

BD776 *(Hurricane II as WG-F)*
KB387 - [12] *(Mosquito XXV)*
KB440 - [1] *(Mosquito XXV)*
RV297 - [58] *(Mosquito XVI)*

M5-G

PF401 - [34], PF462 - [10]
(Mosquito XVI)

M5-H

BE688 *(Hurricane II - letter only)*
PF404 - [28], PF440 - [45]
(Mosquito XVI)

M5-I

M5-J

PF405 - [63] *(Mosquito XVI)*

M5-K

MM194 - [23], RV302 - [44]
(Mosquito XVI)

M5-L

PF410 - [6+*16 as M5-E*] *(Mosquito XVI)*

M5-M

M5-N

M5-O

M5-P

BD897 *(Hurricane II as WG-P)*
KB199 - [6] *(Mosquito XX)*
MM197 - [2], MM198 - [11]
(Mosquito XVI)

M5-Q

MM196 - [12], MM199 - [25 + *1 as M5-U*]
(Mosquito XVI)

M5-R

MM192 - [63 + *1 as M5-W*], RV345 - [15]
(Mosquito XVI)

M5-S

KB403 - [12] *(Mosquito XXV)*
MM223 - [63], PF432 - [1 + *41 as M5-W*]
(Mosquito XVI)

M5-T

PF403 - [33], PF449 [45] *(Mosquito XVI)*

M5-U

KB363 - [14+*14 as M5-C*] *(Mosquito XX)*
MM199 [1 + *25 as M5-Q*], MM203 [2],
PF457 - [25], RV306 - [8] *(Mosquito XVI)*

M5-V

KB449 - [6] *(Mosquito XXV)*
MM202 - [58], RV354 - [13]
(Mosquito XVI)

M5-W

KB425 - [6] *(Mosquito XXV)*
MM192 [1 + *63 as M5-R*],
PF406 - [13 + *22 as M5-E*],
PF432 - [41 + *1 as M5-S*]
(Mosquito XVI)

M5-X

KB395 - [26] *(Mosquito XXV)*
MM204 - [42], MM220 [19]
(Mosquito XVI)

M5-Y

KB399 - [3] *(Mosquito XXV)*
MM201 - [3], PF413 - [60]
(Mosquito XVI)

M5-Z

KB353 - [11] *(Mosquito XX)*
PF409 - [43], PF458 - [28]
(Mosquito XVI)

underlined: Western Africa
in brakets: nbr of take-offs for an operational sortie
Unidentified: One Mosquito XVI mission, and the
assigned letter of KB442 (Mosquito XXV)

RAAF

E.W. **Armstrong**, Aus.433149 (N)
A.J. **Casey**, Aus.432482 (N)
H.R. **Chilvers**, Aus.434404 (N)
G.B. **Collins**, Aus.436900 (N)
E.W.G. **Denton**, Aus.1997 (N)
A.J. **Fawcett**, Aus.409197 (N)
J.F. **Flowers**, Aus.430652 (N)
A.W. **Heitmann**, Aus.409918
P.B. **Jackson**, Aus.409836
N.M. **McNulty**, Aus.409062
D.R. **Murphy**, Aus.433307 (N)
E.P. **O'Malley**, Aus.431260 (N)
A.E. **Parry**, Aus.406661
J.F. **Read**, Aus.413794
K.B. **Sellick**, Aus.407755
K.J.W. **Stump**, Aus.439920 (N)
D.H. **Swain**, Aus.410791
G.W. **Tuck**, Aus.408938
J.B. **Watchorn**, Aus.408117
G.W. **Waugh**, Aus.403232
O.V.S. **Whitshire**, Aus.413922 (N)
J.K. **Wood**, Aus.410777

RAF

O. **Abdullah**, RAF No.1387013 (N)
T.J.S. **Adam**, RAF No.150225, *Australia*
J.C. **Adey**, raf No.1271700
M.J. **Ahearne**, RAF No.119658
R.C. **Alabaster**, RAF No.81065
R.N.G. **Allen**, RAF No.63484
L.G. **Anderson**, RAF No.72090
C.M. **Arrietta**, RAF No.155919 (N)
R.E. **Bain**, RAF No.177423 (N)
N.K. **Bale**, RAF No.1209184
R.G. **Balls**, RAF No.136437
E.D.T. **Barff**, RAF No.657987
D.H. **Basset-Jones**, RAF No.1835962 (N)
J.S. **Batchelor**, RAF No.174775
M.H.A.T. **Bayon**, RAF No.188908 (N)
F. **Belfitt**, RAF No.52178 (N)
A.J. **Benning**, RAF No.1320537
I.L. **Berry**, RAF No.141866
F.W. **Bevis**, RAF No.1654268 (N)
D. **Bird**, RAF No.165532 (N)
F.J. **Blake**, RAF No.150032
H.E. **Boulter**, RAF No.174875
H. **Bradshaw**, RAF No.1589195 (N)
R.W. **Bray**, RAF No.113927
D.W. **Brittan**, RAF No.1587323 (N)
I.J. **Broom**, RAF No.112392
T.J. **Broom**, RAF No.55227 (N)
G.Y. **Broome**, RAF No.143751
A. **Brown**, RAF No.530644 (N)

J. **Brown**, RAF No.1629406 (N)
A.T. **Buckland**, RAF No.68169
R.J. **Burrough**, RAF No.33107
R.M. **Bush**, RAF No.101038
T.N. **Butcher**, RAF No.169481 (N)
N.F. **Byatt**, RAF No.173975
S.W. **Carr**, RAF No.1609352 (N)
L.A. **Chennell**, RAF No.125429
M.R.L. **Chetwynd-Stapylton**,
    RAF No.102064
J.R. **Churcher**, RAF No.1803850 (N)
L. **Clarke**, RAF No.68757
J. **Clements**, RAF No.178772
R.G. **Cook**, RAF No.121407
D.G. **Cooper**, RAF No.179988
W.L. **Cooper**, RAF No.178062
A.H. **Cope**, RAF No.1809047 (N)
K. **Crabtree**, RAF No.1239998
E.W. **Crisp**, RAF No.135646
H.P. **Crumplin**, RAF No.155930 (N)
K.A. **Darley**, RAF No.46873
G.E. **Davies**, RAF No.175823
M.P. **Davis**, RAF No.119872
A.J. **Dawson**, RAF No.1605667 (N)
R.C. **Dempsey**, RAF No.1670369 (N)
J. **Dixon**, RAF No.141521
B. **Drake**, RAF No.39095
D. **Draper**, RAF No.123106
P.J. **Duncan**, RAF No.83994
A. **Dunn**, RAF No.122480
A.M. **Earl**, RAF No.1337480 (N)
F. **Edgard**, RAF No.1026434
D.A. **Edwards**, RAF No.110575
J.L. **Ellis**, RAF No.39510
R.A. **Elson**, RAF No.1584612 (N)
J.S. **Etherington**, RAF No.130645
A. **Fotheringham**, RAF No.173921
J.E. **Fisher**, RAF No.1803471 (N)
S.C. **Fitzsimon**, RAF No.1394392 (N)
J.E. **Foley**, RAF No.190346 (N)
D. **Gallanders**, RAF No.43446
C.A. **Gallifant**, RAF No.125510
J.E. **Genth**, RAF No.116402
G.O.J. **Glover**, RAF No.1801744 (N)
R.G. **Goddard**, RAF No.157109
K.M. **Gosling**, RAF No.127242
A.N. **Gould**, RAF No.188552 (N)
G.W. **Graham**, RAF No.1568003 (N)
B.K. **Green**, RAF No.174640
W.J.C. **Green**, RAF No.190909 (N)
A.L. **Greig**, RAF No.56064
N.E. **Hancock**, RAF No.83266
J. **Harbottle**, RAF No.141809 (N)
D. **Harper**, RAF No.191838 (N)

C.M. **Harrison**, RAF No.118127
S. **Harrison**, RAF No.171806 (N)
C. **Hart**, RAF No.1583265 (N)
D.F.W. **Hart**, RAF No.1807147 (N)
J.L. **Hartley**, RAF 954358 (N)
N.S. **Harvey**, RAF No.1213567
J.J. **Henshaw**, RAF No.120790
J.A. **Henslow**, RAF No.1809686 (N)
C.C. **Hevan**, RAF No.172095 (N)
K.J. **Hicks**, RAF No.166319 (N)
C.C. **Hill**, RAF No.191830 (N)
O.D. **Hill**, RAF No.988499
E.J. **Howes**, RAF No.159924 (N)
T.V. **Hoyle**, RAF No.181158 (N)
W.E.G. **Humphrey**, RAF No.127889
W. **Humphries**, RAF No.156091
A.E. **Hutchinson**, RAF No.115585
A.K.E. **Ibbett**, RAF No.152114
J. **Inkson**, RAF No.146919
A.E. **Jefferson**, RAF No.178721
J.E. **Jenkins**, RAF No.652991
N.C. **Jenkins**, RAF No.1323424 (N)
W.J. **Jinks**, RAF No.128085
B.T.S. **Jones**, RAF No.137095
C.L. **Jones**, RAF No.1607569 (N)
L.J. **Jones**, RAF No.181540 (N)
B.S.B. **Johnston**, RAF No.88475
F.J. **Kaye**, RAF No.100596
R. **Kemp**, RAF No.177974 (N)
C.H. **Kerr**, RAF No.1328028 (N)
P. **Ketley**, RAF No.1625340 (N)
J.I. **Kilmartin**, RAF No.39793, *Ireland*
K. **King**, RAF No.149202
S. **Laycock**, RAF No.1675232 (N)
M.J.L. **Lagesse**, RAF No.128616 (N),
    Mauritius
W. **Lane**, RAF No.197041 (N)
J.E. **Lewis**, RAF No.2220940 (N)
A. **Marder**, RAF No.591731
W.T. **Mayson**, RAF No.148757 (N)
J.C. **McGeagh**, RAF No.170231
R.J. **McIntosh**, RAF No.2204137 (N)
F.L.A. **Morris**, RAF No.143491 (N)
L.C. **Morris**, RAF No.1199897
P.A. **Mortimer**, RAF No.87382
M.H. **Moss**, RAF No.1686131 (N)
G.P. **Mullan**, RAF No.132984 (N)
C. de B. **Newcomb**, RAF No.1382089
R.C. **Onley**, RAF No.102560
C.D. **Owen**, RAF No.45945
W.C. **Parker**, RAF No.1082388 (N)
J.F. **Paterson**, RAF No.1568689 (N)
S.J. **Pearce**, RAF No.169573
F.S. **Pemberton**, RAF No.147271

J.C. **Pickford**, RAF No.1385496 (N)
W.H. **Pithers**, RAF No.181686 (N)
R. **Poole**, RAF No.162285 (N)
N.H. **Prior**, RAF No.189208
W. **Read**, RAF No.174154
A.H. **Reynolds**, RAF No.172379
A.L. **Rhodes**, RAF No.1800829 (N)
D.W. **Rhys**, RAF No.143234
J.A. **Richards**, RAF No.120868
D. **Robb**, RAF No.1671635 (N)
A.W. **Robinson**, RAF No.150114
E.E. **Rodley**, RAF No.61472
L. **Rosser**, RAF No.177862
D.H. **Russell**, RAF No.1605666 (N)
H.a'B. **Russell**, RAF No.37692
E.J. **Saunders**, RAF No.108137 (N)
T.W. **Savage**, RAF No.105167
G.D. **Secretan**, RAF No.155459
E. **Shipley**, RAF No.157822 (N)
C.J. **Smart**, RAF No.1608647 (N)
A.R. **Smith**, RAF No.172871 (N)
J.W.G. **Smith**, RAF No.134129
T.G. **Smith**, RAF No.46347
M.V. **Solomon**, RAF No.144039
R. **Soutar**, RAF No.1672449 (N)
S.R. **Stanbridge**, RAF No.134653 (N)
J.D. **Stewart**, RAF No.1568901 (N)
A.H. **Stuchberry**, RAF No.931711
A.G. **Todd**, RAF No.119873
R.F.L. **Tong**, RAF No.63484
J.W. **Turner**, RAF No.144394
E.P. **Wallace**, RAF No.133403
J.S. **Walter**, RAF No.118970
W.I. **Warmington**, RAF No.150280
L.C.R. **Wellstead**, RAF No.133927

H.W. **Westwood**, RAF No.1584303 (N)
C. **Whittaker**, RAF No.1524097 (N)
P. **Wicks**, RAF No.106614
L.G. **Wilde**, RAF No.1606056 (N)
A.E. **Willey**, RAF No.159877
L.H.J. **Wise**, RAF No.182780 (N)
L.J.I. **Woodward**, RAF No.1604118
A.J.H. **Wright**, RAF No.106161

RCAF

H.J. **Bartley**, Can./J.17039
G.L. **Bikz**, Can./.R.90785
D.J. **Boyer**, Can./J.16118
P.G. **Forcey**, Can./J.8388
T.H. **Hough**, Can./R.64684
F.J. **Kennelly**, Can./J.43629 (N)
A.J. **Kerr**, Can./R.190829 (N)
W.C. **Laing**, Can./R.78739
J.J **Lapointe**, Can./R.62844
J. **Leckenby**, Can./J.43893 (N)
J.R.A. **Maconachie**, Can./C.12525 (N)
B.D. **McEwan**, Can./J.38574
W.R. **McRae**, Can/J.4913
M.J.H. **Murphy**, Can./R.185419 (N)
J.A. **O'Brian**, Can./J.10999
J.C. **Parker**, Can./J.8386
W.A. **Thompson**, Can./R.88744
G.L. **Scott**, Can./J.25988 (N)
A.E. **Shaerer**, Can./J.38202 (N)
J.C. **Schwandt**, Can./J.94302 (N)

RNZAF

B.J. **Caldwell**, NZ421015
G.K. **Doods**, NZ421929 (N)
R.M. **Dwerryhouse**, NZ411868 (N)

T.A. **Empson**, NZ414606
F.W. **Gatley**, NZ431259 (N)
A.J. **Mayfield**, NZ417084
S.M. **McGregor**, NZ413947
L.G. **Porter**, NZ391019
H.C. **Saward**, NZ411943
F.H. **Sherley**, NZ4310390
L.G. **Smith**, NZ4194352
A.R. **Speirs**, NZ413136
R.G. **Webster**, NZ412293
C.B. **Whitmore**, NZ439356
D.M. **Whitney**, NZ391885
A.J. **Woodgate**, NZ412300

SAAF

R.B. **Hart**, SAAF No.205792V
M.H. **Short**, SAAF No.203138V

underlined: Western Africa
(N): Navigators

Note: Roster up to 20.09.45.

APPENDIX IX
ROLL OF HONOUR
✝

AIRCREW

Name	Service No	Rank	Age	Origin	Date	Serial
ADAM, Treless James Stewart	RAF No.150225	F/O	28	(AUS)/RAF	14.01.45	PF404
ARMSTRONG, John David	CAN./J.5707	S/L	30	RCAF	07.03.45	RV306
BRITTAN, Donald William	RAF No.1587323	Sgt	23	RAF	07.11.44	KB353
CABELDU, James Norman	CAN./R.99147	Sgt	25	RCAF	19.11.42	BE550
CASEY, Allan James	AUS.432482	F/Sgt	23	RAAF	14.01.45	PF404
COLLINS, George Barrowby	AUS.436900	F/O	19	RAAF	11.12.44	MM190
EDGAR, Frank	RAF No.1026434	W/O	24	RAF	29.11.44	MM195
ELLIS, Jack Llewelyn	RAF No.39510	F/L	n/k	RAF	07.11.44	KB353
HARTLEY, John Leonard	RAF No.954358	Sgt	24	RAF	17.09.44	KB210
HEITMANN, Alan Walter	AUS.409918	F/L	23	RAAF	15.01.45	MM194
KING, Kenneth Henry	RAF No.149202	F/O	21	RAF	31.10.44	KB199
LAGESSE, Marie Joseph Marc[1]	RAF No.128616	F/L	27	RAF	10.01.45	PF403
MACONACHIE, James Roy Alexander	CAN./C.12525	F/O	34	RCAF	28.02.45	PF451
MARDER, Allan	RAF No.591731	Sgt	19	RAF	24.05.42	BN223
McNULTY, Neville Milne	AUS.409062	F/O	29	RAAF	28.02.45	PF451
MOSS, Maurice Henry	RAF No.1686131	Sgt	n/k	RAF	24.11.44	MM201
MULLAN, George Patrick	RAF No.132984	F/L	33	RAF	01.01.45	PF411
MURPHY, Joseph Harold Michael	CAN./J.95450	P/O	22	RCAF	28.11.44	MM195
ONLEY, Ronald Charles	RAF No.102560	F/L	32	RAF	11.12.44	MM190
POOLE, Raymond	RAF No.162285	F/O	n/k	RAF	05.02.45	MM199
TUCK, George William	AUS.408938	F/O	25	RAAF	24.11.44	MM201
SOUTAR, Robert Alexander	RAF No.1672449	Sgt	23	RAF	04.11.44	MM197
TONG, Ronald Frederick Leonard	RAF No.63848	S/L	27	RAF	10.01.45	PF403
WALLACE, Edward Peter	RAF No.133403	F/O	21	RAF	04.11.44	MM197
WELLSTEAD, Leo Charles Raymond	RAF No.133927	F/L	22	RAF	01.01.45	PF414
WHYTE, William Edward	CAN./J.42207	F/O	21	RCAF	07.03.45	RV306
WOOD, James Knox	AUS.410777	F/L	23	RAAF	05.02.45	MM199

[1] From Mauritius

Total: 27
Australia: 6, Canada: 5, United Kingdom: 15

GROUNDCREW

Name	Service No	Rank	Age	Origin	Date	Serial
BAKER, Cyril	RAF No.573603	AC1	19	RAF	23.11.41	-
MAHON, Joseph William	RAF No.1354267	LAC	35	RAF	04.12.42	-
SELL, Jeffery	RAF No.633387	LAC	20	RAF	20.07.42	-

Total: 3
United Kingdom: 3

n/k: not known

In 1941 -1942 and especially overseas, the Hurricane was the main fighter the RAF could deploy. As the French had no fighters in the area, the Hurricane could not expect to face a dangerous enemy and anyway the Hurricane was perfectly suited to intercept the French reconnaissance aircraft. Here is Hurricane BD776/WG-F on patrol at the end 1941. Note that, to avoid any mistake with the French roundels, the spinners were also painted in RAF roundel colours, even if the French aircraft were flying with the Vicky orange/yellow stripes. This practice seems to have been discontinued in 1942. Below, maintenance of one of the few Hurricanes in service by 1941. The hot and humid African climate was tough and it was not an easy task for the groundcrew. However they were able to maintain enough Hurricanes for the job, knowing that a regular lack of spares didn't help that much either in the beginning. In December 1941, the squadron was flying two Hurricane Mk.Is (Z4313 and Z4484) inherited from No.95 Sqn Defense Flight, later joined by Hurricane IIBs BD897 and BD876 by the end of October 1941. In November, Hurricane Mk.I Z4256 was added, but by April 1942 enough Hurricanes Mk.IIs were available and the Mk.Is were relegated to training duties with the squadron. When No.128 Sqn was disbanded, except for Z4484 which was used by No.208 Sqn, it seems that all the other Mk.Is were stored and never used again. It is believed that Z4484 was locally modified to carry out photographic reconnaissance flights, hence its later use by No.208 Sqn. If so, Z4484 was replaced by Hurricane Mk.II Z2420, also locally modified with cameras and painted in light or PR blue.

In spring 1942, the squadron needed a complement of aircraft to equip the newly-formed B Flight and from April 1942 onwards obtained Hurricanes Mk.IIs including BE688 - H and BH217 - A (right). They served until disbandment of the unit in 1943. Note that the squadron code 'WG' was discontinued by that time. In 1943, the following Hurricanes were also in use at Hastings: Z4256, Z5217, Z5340, AG297, BD897, BH126, BH279, BN603, HV784, HV785, HV821, HV822, HV891, HV892, HV893, HV900, HV901, HW183

It also is believed that BD776 and BH219 were locally modified to carry cameras.

Above: The Mosquito Mk.XVI had become by 1944 the mainstay of the Mosquito Pathfinder force of Bomber Command and had supplanted all the other bomber versions. The last bomber version to be put into service during the war, it performed well and gave excellent results with a low loss rate ratio. Above the squadron is taxying for another mission over Germany, PF443/M5-A leading. This Mosquito was usually flown by the New Zealander crew F/L Thomas Empson, pilot and F/O Robert Dwerryhouse, navigator. Thirty mission markings can be seen under the cockpit, giving the indication that this picture was taken around the end of March 1945. The crew survived and was awarded the DFC, while PF443 added about a dozen more sorties to its tally.

Below, another high scoring squadron Mosquito, RV297/M5-F, which was taken on squadron charge in December 1944. Up to the end of war, it recorded close to 60 sorties. Early in 1945, it was generally flown by the crew F/L William E.G. Humphrey, pilot who had been awarded the DFC while serving with No.105 Sqn and his navigator F/O Trevor Butcher who was awarded the DFC in May 1945 for his service with the squadron. However, by the end of war RV297 had changed its crew, being usually flown by F/O Norman Byatt, pilot, and his Australian navigator, F/Sgt Edward O'Malley.

No.128 Sqn counted a number of very experienced pilots in its roster, starting with the first CO, Billy Drake, posing here in his Hurricane with which he shot down a French Glenn Martin in December 1941. Even if the Martin 167 was probably only damaged, as no loss is recorded in the French archives, the claim was confirmed and was given much publicity to help the French to keep away from Hastings and its area - hence the photo above. Drake was a Londoner, who had joined the RAF in July 1936 and by the outbreak of war he was flying with No.1 Sqn and was stationed in France when the Germans launched their offensive in May 1940. He had previously opened his score on 20 April in shooting down a Bf109. He then participated to the Battle of France and after more successes he was wounded in action while fighting against Bf110s. After recovery he was briefly posted to No.213 Sqn and later to No.421 Flight on its formation. By the end of 1940 he had completed his tour and was posted to an OTU, with a DFC. In September 1941 he was sent to West Africa and took command of the squadron and in April 1942, he was posted to the Western Desert where joined No.112 Sqn with which he achieved considerable success. He left the unit at the end of 1942, and was posted to Malta in June 1943 to take over Krendi Wing. Later in 1944 he returned to the UK and led a Typhoon Wing until spring 1944. He ended the war with 24.5 confirmed victories, 9 more probables and the DFC & Bar. He remained with the RAF after the war until he retired in 1963.

Australian-born New Zealander Douglas M. Whitney was another experienced pilot. He enlisted in August 1939 in the RNZAF and by August 1940 he had joined No.245 Sqn with which he fought during the Battle of Britain, later serving with No.17 Sqn. At the end of 1940, he volunteered to serve overseas and served briefly with No.261 Sqn in March-April 1941 with which he claimed two Bf109s destroyed. In the autumn, he joined the squadron in formation and stayed with the unit until November 1942 (except for two months between March and June 1942). He was repatriated to New Zealand in June 1943 where he served as flying instructor until the end of war.
(D.M. Whitney via Paul Sortehaug)

Some of the squadron's pilots in 1942:
Unknown, P/O Maurice Davies who survived the war, unknown, F/L Douglas Whitney and P/O Todd. Arthur Todd was previously a member of No.95 Sqn Defense Flight and was responsible for the destruction of the first French aircraft, a Martin 167, on 22.08.41. He had previously flown with No.245 Sqn in the UK, then with No.261 Sqn in Malta. He returned to the UK at the end of 1942 and after a rest he started another tour of operations with No.56 Sqn on Typhoons, joining later No.164 Sqn with which he claimed two confirmed victories, both being shared. A third tour followed in 1945 as CO of No.257 Sqn.
(D.M. Whitney via Paul Sortehaug)

When he left for the Middle East, Squadron Leader Drake relinquished command to the Irish-born John I. Kilmartin (left), another experienced pilot who had joined No.95 Sqn Defense Flight in June 1941. 'Killy' Kilmartin was a pre-war RAF pilot and was serving with No.43 Sqn when war broke out. In November 1939 he joined No.1 Sqn based in France (where Drake became his squadron mate) and open his score by sharing the destruction of a Do17 on the 23th. He participated in the Battle of France and when he returned to the UK at the end of May 1940, he had added 13 more victories (one being shared). After a short rest at an OTU, he returned to combat during the Battle of Britain with No.43 Sqn as a Flight Commander and shot down two Bf109s in September 1940, being awarded a DFC the following month. After another short rest, he was posted to No.602 Sqn as CO in April 1941 but soon afterwards he was posted to the new-formed No.313 (Czech) Sqn to help to building up this unit. In June he was sailing to Western Africa where he joined No.95 Sqn Defense Flight. After his stay with No.128 Sqn, he returned to the UK to lead No.504 Sqn first, then the Hornchurch Wing. In 1944 he participated in D-Day by leading No.136 Wing on Typhoons, but was posted to HQ - No.2 TAF after the disbandment of the Wing in June 1945. He returned overseas to take command of No.910 Wing (Thunderbolts) in Burma but the war ended before any major sortie was carried out. He remained with the RAF until 1958, when he retired as a Wing Commander.

Right, another DFC holder, P/O Robert Allen, who became the only squadron member to be awarded the DFC while serving in Western Africa. Allen became the reconnaissance pilot of the squadron and carried out most of the reconnaissance sorties flying the locally modified Hurricanes or even the single Spitfire IV used by the squadron.

If finding a crew with its members named 'Smith' during the war it rather easy, it was less common to have two 'Brooms' flying together, although they were not relatives. Left Ivor G. Broom, pilot and his navigator, Thomas 'Tommy' Broom. This crew flew no less than 58 missions together flying 8 Group Mosquitoes of Nos.571, 128 and 163 Sqns. Ivor Broom continued his RAF career after the war and later became Air Marshal Sir Ivor Broom, KCB CBE DSO DFC two Bars AFC. While serving No.128 Sqn, Ivor Broom was awarded a second bar to his DFC (after a DFC in 1942 - No.107 Sqn - and a Bar in 1944 - No.571 Sqn -), while Thomas Broom was awarded a first Bar to his DFC awarded in 1944 while flying with No.571 Sqn. He later added a second Bar in 1945 whilst flying with No.163 Sqn.

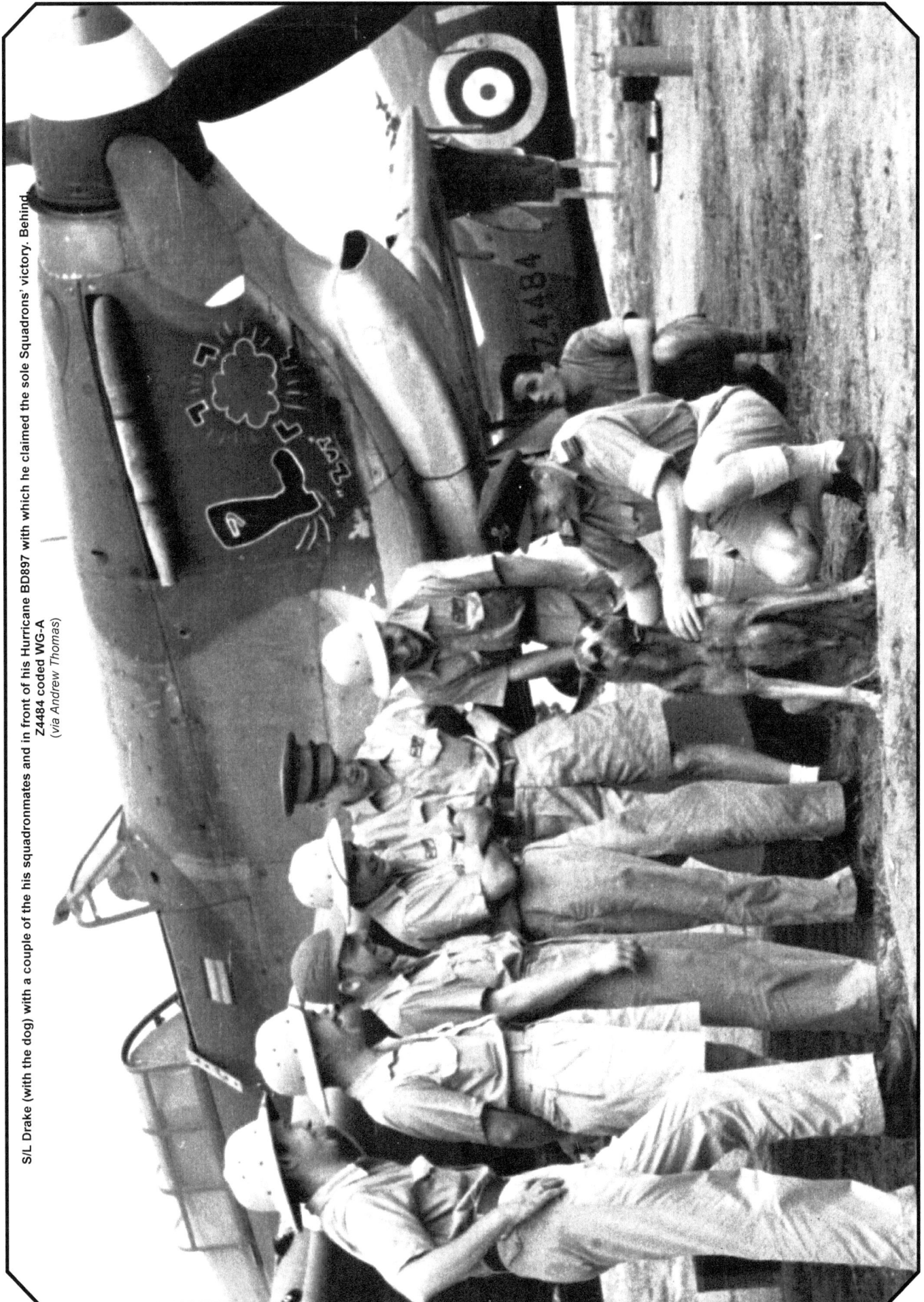

S/L Drake (with the dog) with a couple of the his squadronmates and in front of his Hurricane BD897 with which he claimed the sole Squadrons' victory. Behind, Z4484 coded **WG-A**
(via Andrew Thomas)

Summary of the operational activity
No.128 Squadron

A/C types	First sortie	Last sortie	Total sorties	Tot Sub-type	Lost Ops	Lost Acc	A/C lost	Claims	Pilot †	PoWs	Eva.
HURRICANE I& II [1]	13.12.41	27.01.43	301	301	1	4	5	1	2	-	-
SPITFIRE IV	?	?	?	?	1	-	-	-	-	-	-
MOSQUITO XX	10.09.44	18.11.44	104	104	3	-	3	-	4	1	-
MOSQUITO XXV	03.10.44	29.11.44	85	85	-	-	-	-	-	-	-
MOSQUITO XVI	23.10.44	02.05.45	1,262	1,262	17	5	22	-	21	-	-
OTHER CAUSES	-	-	-	-	-	-	-	-	-	-	-
COMPILATION	13.12.41	02.05.45	1,752	-	21	9	30	1.0	27	1	-

[1] The exact breakdown can't be determined with certitude but at least 7 Hurricane Mk.Is sorties can be identified.

MAIN AWARDS

DSO: 1

DFC: 37

DFM: 3

Points of interest:
None.

Unsolved mystery:
Unidentified pilots: Sgt Kirkup (1941-42), Sgt S.T. Parker (May 42), P/O A.H. McLaren (Oct 1942) - Sgt T. Alexander (Jan-43)

Statistics: (Mosquito only)
- Lost one aircraft every 76 sorties (35 for Mosquito XXs - 79 Mosquito XVIs).
- 24.00 % of the combat aircraft losses occurred during non operational flights.

BADGE
In front of an ogress a shuttle in hand.

The badge refers to the squadron's period as a Mosquito bomber squadron, the ogress signifying night operations and the shuttle imlying regularity.

MOTTO
FULMINIS INSTAR

LIKE A THUNDERBOLT

Authority: King George VI, March 1946

Hawker Hurricane Mk.IIB/Trop. BD776, Hastings, Sierra Leone, December 1941.
Buit by Hawker, BD776 was taken on by the RAF at No.48 MU on 22.08.41. It was earmarked to serve in the Middle East and sent to No.58 MU on 28.08.41 probably for tropicalisation. It was shipped out to the Middle East on 03.09.41. The photo of this aircraft is published p.18. When formed, the squadron had to fill in its aircraft complement with available aircraft and diverted some Hurricanes from their original destination. Hence BD776 was uncrated and sent to No.3 Hangar for assembly on 26.10.41 and flew with this camouflage (Tropical Land Scheme) at least for a while but it is not known with certainty if it was repainted or not, but it might have been locally modified to carry cameras. It was used by the squadron until disbandment and eventually ferried out to the Middle East in March 1943, its original destination. After having been stored for a while it was sold to the Turkish Air Force on 01.07.43.

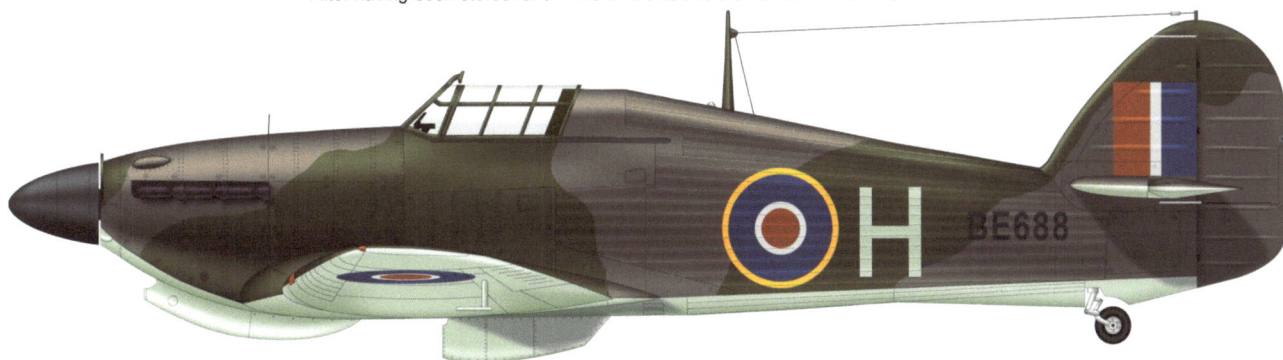

Hawker Hurricane Mk.IIB/Trop. BE688, Hastings, Sierra Leone, Autumn 1942.
Taken on RAF charge on 15.11.41 at No.19 MU in UK it was stored before being sent to Western Africa on 09.03.42 where it arrived on 06.05.42. Immediately assembled, it was issued to No.128 Sqn a couple of days later and a first flight was recorded on 10.05.42. It was painted in Tropical Land Scheme (Dark Green/Dark Earth and believed Sky Blue for undersurfaces) which was more suitable to the landscape of Western Africa compared to former Hurricanes used by the squadron. It seems that in March 1943, BE688 was sent to the Middle East, but subsequent allocation is not confirmed by any kind of record. It was eventually struck off charge in October 1945.

Hawker Hurricane Mk.IIB/Trop. BD897, S/L Billy Drake, Hastings, Sierra Leone, December 1941.

BD897 had a similar history to BD776, as it was taken on RAF charge on 04.08.41 at No.5 MU and probably tropicalised at No.52 MU from 29.08.41. It was sent the same day as BD776 and it is believed that it was uncrated at Hastings on 18.10.41. It became the mount of the CO, hence the Squadron Leader pennant, and while flying this aircraft, Drake claimed a French Martin 167 on 13.12.41. This claim was highly publicised and many photos taken after that date. As for BD776, it was eventually ferried out to the Middle East in March 1943. If it was used until March 1943, the fact that it was repainted is not proved even if it is likely the case. The true fate of this Hurricane remains obscure and no trace of this aircraft was found after April 43. It is possible that it was stored and never used again and was officially struck off charge on 01.01.47, an administrative date which suggests a loss of follow-up soon after its arrival in the Middle East.

Hawker Hurricane Mk.IIB BH217, Hastings (Sierra Leone), Autumn 1942.

BH217 had a career similar to BE688. It was taken on RAF charge on 06.01.42 at No.19 MU, it was crated to be sent overseas on 12.03.42 and reached Takoradi on board SS *Katanga* a couple of weeks later. Assembled, it was issued to No.128 Sqn and a first flight was recorded on 25.05.42. By 01.04.43 it had been ferried out to the Middle East and later used by No.1571 Flt in Ceylon for a while. It was eventually struck off charge on 27.10.44.

De Havilland Mosquito B.XVI PF401, S/L Ivor G. Broom & F/L Thomas G. Broom, Wyton, United Kingdom, end 1944.
Built by Percival Aircraft, PF401 was one of the first Mosquito B.XVIs to be taken on charge by the squadron in October 1944 and carried out the first No.128 Sqn Mosquito B.XVI sortie on 23.10.44 with the crew of S/L I.G. Broom & F/L T.G. Broom on board. This aircraft became the regular mount of this crew but they weren't flying PF401 when it crashed on landing returning from Berlin (see operational losses). It had just completed its 34ᵗʰ sortie.

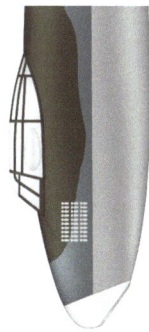

sample of bomb markings used on 128 Sqn Mosquitos

De Havilland Mosquito B.XVI PF443, F/L Thomas Empson (RNZAF) & F/O Robert Dwerryhouse (RNZAF), Wyton, United Kingdom, March 1945.
Built by Percival Aircraft in 1944, PF443 was stored until 15.01.45 when it was allocated to No.105 Sqn. However it stayed with this unit a short time as it was reported to be with No.128 Sqn on 23.01.45. It was from then regularly flown by the New-Zealander crew F/L Empson & F/O Dwerryhouse and PF443 flew its first operation on 28.01.45 adding 44 others until its last recorded one on 25.04.45 (see provisional bomb markings painted on the nose seen on the photo in March 1945). PF443 continued to fly with No.128 Sqn and later with No.14 Sqn when the squadron was renamed and was stored on 11.11.47 to be sold for scrap in August 1948.

USN AIRCRAFT
1922-

Fighter Leaders
of the RAF, RAAF, RCAF, RNZAF & SAAF in WW2

The Supermarine
SPITFIRE Mk.V
in the Far East

Volume I

Phil H. Listemann

RAF, DOMINION & ALLIED SQUADRONS
AT WAR:
STUDY, HISTORY AND STATISTICS

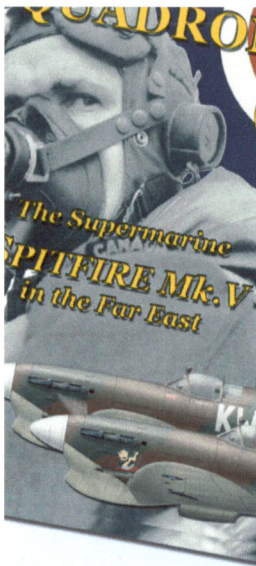

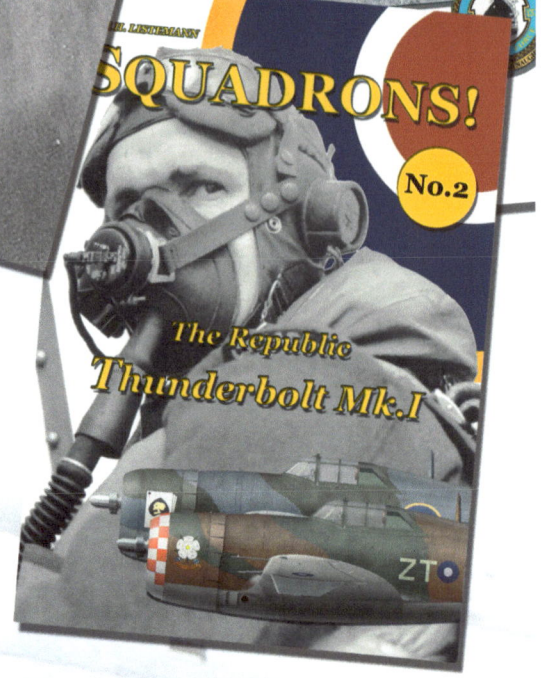

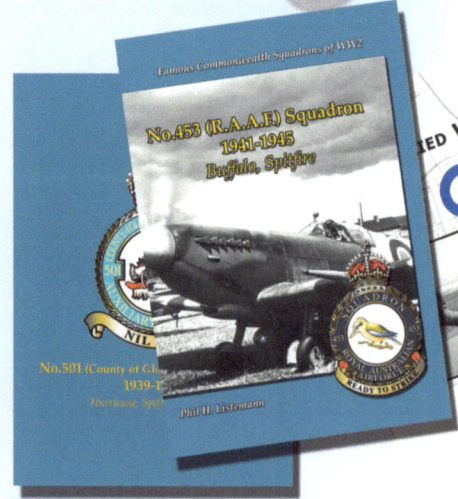

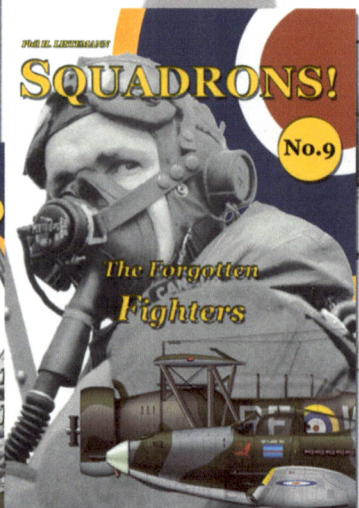

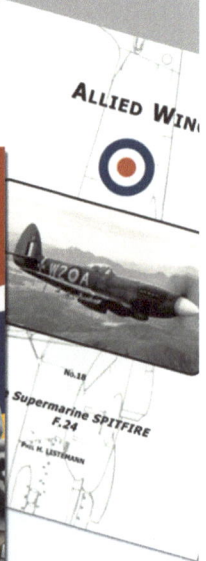

No.137 Squadron
1941 - 1945

SQUADRONS!

No.2

The Republic
Thunderbolt Mk.I

www.RAF-IN-COMBAT.com

- USN Aircraft 1922-1962 -
- Squadrons! -
- RAF, Dominion and Allied squadrons at War -
- Allied Wings -
- Famous squadrons of WW2 -
- Fighter Leaders -

RAF, DOMINION & ALLIED SQUADRONS
AT WAR:
STUDY, HISTORY AND STATISTICS

ALLIED WINGS

Famous Commonwealth Squadrons of WW2

No.453 (R.A.A.F) Squadron
1941-1945
Buffalo, Spitfire

No.131 (County of Kent Squadron
1941 - 1945

ALLIED WINGS

No.501 (County of G...
1939-1...

Phil H. Listemann

Supermarine SPITFIRE
F.24

SQUADRONS!

No.9

The Forgotten
Fighters

The Handley
Halifax

www.ingramcontent.com/pod-product-compliance
Lightning Source LLC
LaVergne TN
LVHW072122070426
835511LV00002B/67